BEGINNING TO READ

1

MARVEL

SPIDER-MAN

The Amazing Story

Catherine Saunders

Hisle

A Note to Parents and Teachers

Dorling Kindersley Readers is a compelling reading programme for beginning readers, designed in conjunction with leading literacy experts, including Cliff Moon, M.Ed., Honorary Fellow of the University of Reading. Cliff Moon has spent many years as a teacher and teacher educator specialising in reading and has written more than 140 books for children and teachers. He reviews regularly for teachers' journals.

Beautiful illustrations and superb full-colour photographs combine with engaging, easy-to-read stories to offer a fresh approach to each subject in the series. Each DK READER is guaranteed to capture a child's interest while developing his or her reading skills, general knowledge and love of reading.

The five levels of DK READERS are aimed at different reading abilities, enabling you to choose the books that are exactly right for your child:

Pre-level 1 – Learning to read
Level 1 – Beginning to read
Level 2 – Beginning to read alone
Level 3 – Reading alone
Level 4 – Proficient readers

The "normal" age at which a child begins to read can be anywhere from three to eight years old, so these levels are intended only as a general guideline.

No matter which level you select, you can be sure that you are helping your child learn to read, then read to learn!

Penguin
Random
House

For DK

Senior Designer David McDonald
Designer Stefan Georgiou
Production Controller Sara Hu
Pre-Production Producer Kavita Varma
Managing Editor Sadie Smith
Design Managers Guy Harvey,
Ron Stobbart
Creative Manager Sarah Harland
Art Director Lisa Lanzarini
Publisher Julie Ferris
Publishing Director Simon Beecroft

Created by Tall Tree Ltd.

Editor Kate Simkins
Designer Ed Simkins

Reading Consultant
Cliff Moon. M.Ed.

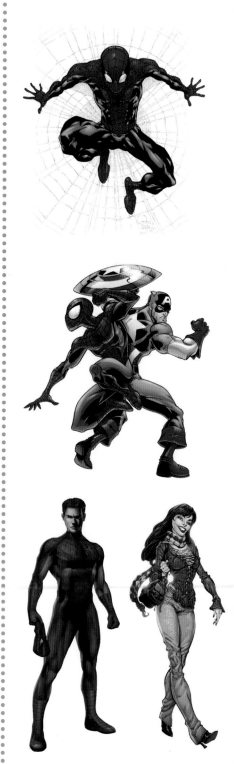

This edition published in 2017
First published in Great Britain in 2006 by
Dorling Kindersley Limited,
80 Strand, London WC2R 0RL
A Penguin Random House Company

027-SD223-Apr/2006

A CIP catalogue record for this book is available from
the British Library.

ISBN 978-1-4053-1406-0

Printed and bound in China

www.dk.com

A WORLD OF IDEAS:
SEE ALL THERE IS TO KNOW

DK READERS

BEGINNING **1** TO READ

MARVEL
SPIDER-MAN
The Amazing Story

Written by Catherine Saunders

Spider-Man's
real name is
Peter Parker.
Peter was
an ordinary
boy.

He lived in New York
City, USA, with
his Aunt May and
Uncle Ben.
Peter often dreamt of
being a Super Hero.

Spider-Man

Peter Parker was a student at
Midtown High School.
He was very clever and worked
hard at his lessons.

He always got good marks and his favourite subject was science.

student

Peter was a quiet, shy boy who did not have many friends.

He was not very good at sport, and he was afraid of heights.

Other students, like Flash Thompson, sometimes made fun of him.

One day, Peter Parker's life changed forever.
He was bitten by a radioactive spider at a science exhibition.

The spider's poison entered
Peter's body and
made him start to change.
He felt very strange!

spider

The spider's bite gave
Peter fantastic new powers.

He became
really strong
and could climb
tall skyscrapers.

skyscrapers

Peter decided to become
a wrestling star on television.
He called himself Spider-Man.

One day, Uncle Ben was killed
by a burglar.
This made Peter decide to use
his amazing powers to help people
and catch criminals.

burglar

BEN PARKER
HE WAS
LOVED

Peter turned Spider-Man
from a television star into
a Super Hero!

Spider-Man's special costume and mask protect his true identity from his enemies.

costume

Peter wears his Spider-Man
costume under his clothes.
He is always ready to leap
into action!

Every spider has a web.
Peter Parker used the science
he learnt in school
to make Spider-Man's web.

Spider-Man shoots the web
from his wrists.
He uses it to swing
from building to building.

web

Spider-Man is always one step
ahead of danger, thanks to
his spider-sense.

He can tell if any of his enemies
are trying to sneak up on him.
His spider-sense even works
in the dark.

Spider-Man has
amazing strength.
He can bend iron bars and
punch through walls.

He can also jump higher
than a house and
leap across the rooftops.

Spider-Man can also think
very quickly.
This makes him good at catching
even the cleverest criminals.

Spider-Man has many enemies,
like the Scorpion and
Doctor Octopus.

Peter Parker is in love with
Mary Jane Watson,
who lives
next door.

Mary Jane likes Peter.
She secretly thinks that
he might be Spider-Man.

Spider-Man usually works alone,
but sometimes even he needs help
from his Super Hero friends.

Daredevil and Captain America
have both helped Spider-Man
to fight crime.

Peter Parker knows that
his powers make him different
from other people.
He believes that Spider-Man must
help people who need him.

Spider-Man does his best
to make the world a safer place.

Picture word list

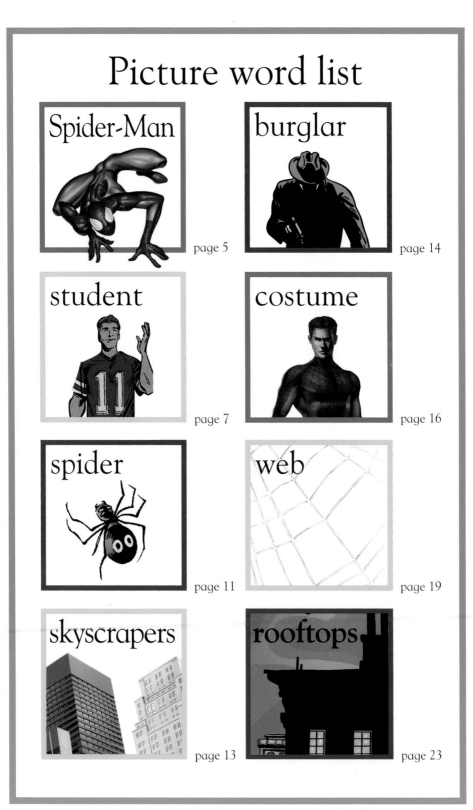

Spider-Man
page 5

burglar
page 14

student
page 7

costume
page 16

spider
page 11

web
page 19

skyscrapers
page 13

rooftops
page 23